W9-BKK-655

say a
little prayer

101 WAYS TO PRAY
THROUGHOUT YOUR DAY

joanne redmond

Our Daily Bread
Publishing.

Say a Little Prayer: 101 Ways to Pray throughout Your Day
© 2023 by Joanne Redmond

All rights reserved.

Say a Little Prayer was previously published under the same title by Marlowe & Company (2004).

Requests for permission to quote from this book should be directed to: Permissions Department, Our Daily Bread Publishing, PO Box 3566, Grand Rapids, MI 49501, or contact us by email at permissionsdept@odb.org.

Scripture quotations, unless otherwise indicated, are taken from the Holy Bible, New International Version®, NIV®. Copyright © 1973, 1978, 1984, 2011 by Biblica, Inc.™ Used by permission of Zondervan. All rights reserved worldwide. www.zondervan.com.

Scripture quotations marked KJV are taken from the Authorized Version, or King James Version, of the Bible.

Scripture quotations marked TLB are taken from *The Living Bible* copyright © 1971. Used by permission of Tyndale House Publishers, Inc., Carol Stream, Illinois 60188. All rights reserved.

Cover design by Patti Brinks

Interior design by Gayle Raymer

Photo credit: Tyler Brown

Internal photographs © 2023 by Carrie Rosema. All rights reserved.

Library of Congress Cataloging-in-Publication Data

Names: Redmond, Joanne, author. | Our Daily Bread (Organization), contributor.
Title: Say a little prayer : 101 ways to pray throughout your day / Joanne Redmond.
Description: Grand Rapids, MI : Our Daily Bread Publishing, [2023] | Summary: "Alongside pictures, Scripture verses, and quotations, Joanne Redmond suggests 101 everyday opportunities to increase your communication with God" -- Provided by publisher.
Identifiers: LCCN 2022050458 | ISBN 9781640702301 | ISBN 9781640702417 (ebook)
Subjects: LCSH: Prayer--Christianity.
Classification: LCC BV215 .R415 2023 | DDC 248.3/2--dc23/eng/20230126
LC record available at https://lccn.loc.gov/2022050458

Printed in China
23 24 25 26 27 28 29 30 / 9 8 7 6 5 4 3 2

To my wonderful colleagues at Kyndryl and IBM. May you each come to know how very much God loves you.

INTRODUCTION

"Boys and girls, when we pray, we bow our heads,
fold our hands, and close our eyes . . ."

Did you ever go to Sunday school as a child? I have vivid memories of being in class one morning as a second grader, listening to our teacher instructing us how to pray. As I sat on one of those gray folding chairs too big for my little body, feet dangling several inches off the ground, I remember thinking, *If I have to keep my hands folded and my eyes closed for one more second, I AM GOING TO BURST!* My active imagination and youthful energy did not make it easy to sit still, and I definitely could not talk to anyone with my eyes closed.

As an adult, I felt guilty having similar feelings of not being able to concentrate while praying. During church, there was usually a moment when someone would lead the congregation in prayer, often for several minutes. Always wanting to say profound things to God, I would start out, "Dear God, thank you so much for this wonderful day, for bringing me here safely, and—" Then my mind would suddenly take off in different directions. One morning I outlined a term paper for graduate school. Another time, I redecorated the living room. Great vacations were planned, monumental decisions made, all in the short span of a leader's prayer. Inevitably, I felt ashamed and chastised myself for my lack of concentration. I knew I was supposed to pray more . . . and not just at church. But I found it to be very *boring*.

Fortunately, with time, I was able to channel my creativity and apply it to my prayer life. Prayer does not need to be dull and monotonous! It can be the most dynamic, exciting aspect of life. After all, we have the privilege of connecting with the Author and Creator of the entire universe.

And He wants to hear from us! He desires to communicate and have a close relationship with me and with you.

The Bible says to "pray without ceasing." The apostle Paul certainly did not mean we should spend the entire day walking around with our heads bowed, hands folded, and eyes closed, the way I learned in Sunday school. This book is designed to give you one or several creative ideas of how to improve your prayer life—there are *many* ways to talk to God.

Some suggestions may work for you, others may not. As you apply the ideas most meaningful to you, I pray that you may have a more vibrant and fulfilling prayer life.

"Ev'ry time I feel
de Spirit movin' in my
heart, I will pray."

AFRICAN-AMERICAN SPIRITUAL

1

While brushing your teeth in the morning, pray for three things you need help with during the day.

Thanks be to thee, my Lord Jesus Christ,
for all the benefits thou hast given me,
for all the pains and insults thou hast
    borne for me.
O most merciful redeemer, friend and
    brother,
may I know thee more clearly,
love thee more dearly,
and follow thee more nearly, day by day.
Amen.

ST. RICHARD OF CHICHESTER,
ENGLISH BISHOP, 1197–1253

2

If prayer is very difficult for you, plan one time during the week when you will pray only one sentence. Be very specific about the exact place and time that you will pray. That brief moment can gradually change your life.

"The wish to pray is a prayer in itself. . . . God can ask no more than that of us."

GEORGES BERNANOS,
FRENCH NOVELIST, 1888–1948

3

Any time you use a credit card or pay for a purchase using your mobile device, ask God for discernment in spending your money.

guidance

4

Tend to react when you feel angry? Pray to develop the ability to STOP, THINK, and SEE the situation from the other person's point of view before responding.

5

Before reading
the Bible, ask God to
reveal Himself to you
through His Word.

6

Sometimes, the sense of love for a child can be so strong that it's hard to express—but you can still connect to God during these times. You can look up and smile, or simply tell God that you're feeling so much love you can't put it into words.

love

7

Write your prayers on a personal computer or smartphone. Some people can type almost as quickly as they can talk, and they find it easier to concentrate when their fingers are moving.

Here is a suggested template for a prayer written on your computer or phone:

Dear Father,

Paragraph 1: List things you're thankful for

Paragraph 2: Two or three sentences asking forgiveness (be specific)

Paragraph 3: A few sentences offering praise

Paragraph 4: Requests

Sign your name

8

When reading about or
viewing a troubling situation
in the world, pray for peace
in both the circumstance and
within your heart.

9

When faced with a
delay—a long line,
a missed bus, a late
test result, waiting on
hold—ask for patience.

10

If you want to communicate with God, but feel like the right words are not coming, listen to a song of praise and sing or hum it to Him.

praise

11

If you think you are praying about something the wrong way— say it anyway! God understands what you really mean.

"A grandfather was walking through his yard when he heard his granddaughter repeating the alphabet in a tone of voice that sounded like a prayer. He asked her what she was doing. The little girl explained: 'I'm praying, but I can't think of exactly the right words, so I'm just saying all the letters, and God will put them together for me, because he knows what I'm thinking.'"

CHARLES B. VAUGHAN,
ENGLISH SCHOLAR, 1816–1897

12

When you feel great despair
and are tempted to turn to
a substance such as alcohol
or drugs to numb your pain,
ask God for help.

13

As you put on your pajamas at night, ask God to help you feel relaxed and content.

14

As you pour your morning coffee, ask for help with a painful relationship.

help

15

Think something is too small
to pray for? Pray for it anyway.
Remember, God cares about the
little things—He even knows
how many hairs are on your
head (Matthew 10:30).

Do you have to pray with your eyes closed? No! Both Matthew and John wrote accounts of Christ looking toward heaven when praying.

16

When texting
someone or calling
them on the phone,
ask God to bless
them while you
wait for an answer.

blessing

17

Having trouble
communicating with your
spouse? Ask God to change
his or her heart . . .
and yours.

18

Lose something?
Ask God to help you
find it. Don't forget
to thank Him once
you do.

19

When you are over-whelmed with sadness, place your head on a pillow. Imagine you are resting in God's lap. Pour out your pain to Him.

"Prayer is the burden of a sigh,
The falling of a tear,
The upward glancing of an eye,
When none but God is near."

JAMES MONTGOMERY,
SCOTTISH POET, 1771–1854

20

When you have contact with an elderly relative, thank God for his or her life, and ask God to teach and bless you through your interactions with that person.

gratitude

21

When you're about to share something on social media, ask God to help you pause before you post.

"Let the words of my mouth, and the meditation of my heart, be acceptable in thy sight, O LORD, my strength, and my redeemer."

PSALM 19:14 KJV

22

Before visiting your family of origin, ask God to help you not fall into old behavior patterns or habits, but to practice the maturity and growth you've experienced.

23

Ask God to point out what needs to be changed in your life. Can't think of anything? Just ask Him—He will show you.

24

Go somewhere alone.
Ask God to speak to
you. Sit still, be quiet,
and listen.

listen

25

Pray on your knees.

Here is a suggested guide for things to pray each day of the week:

Sunday: The week ahead

Monday: Your family

Tuesday: Co-workers or those you see daily

Wednesday: Your friends

Thursday: Yourself

Friday: Your country and government leaders

Saturday: An area of the world that is not at peace

26

When you unlock your phone or computer, rather than jumping straight to the activity on your mind, pause and ask God to help you be wise with your time.

wisdom

27

Pray silently as you are in your bed ready to fall asleep. God will not mind if you doze off while talking to Him— there's no better way to fall asleep.

28

When faced with a difficult struggle, write a letter to God. Be sure to date it, so you can read it in the future and see how God was working in your life. Some people choose to keep a list of requests and then leave space in their journals for noting how and when the prayer was answered.

29

When you wake each morning, thank God for your rest and for the day ahead.

"Arise, shine, for your light
has come,
and the glory of the Lᴏʀᴅ
rises upon you."

ISAIAH 60:1

30

Talk to God while loading your dish-washer or drying your dishes.

everyday

31

At times, reading through comments on social media can evoke feelings of anger, despair, frustration and disgust—pray that God's truth would replace the "noise."

32

This may sound irreverent, but some days are so busy or stressful that the only time we have to pray is in the restroom. (When I was single, this one especially came in handy during really bad dates. Then, I found myself praying this way after I became a mom.)

33

Feeling joyful? "Shout for
joy to the LORD, all the earth,
burst into jubilant song
with music."

**KING DAVID OF ISRAEL
(PSALM 98:4)**

"Sing to him, sing praise to him; tell of all his wonderful acts."

PSALM 105:2

34

In your workplace, pray for someone as you pass their office or desk.

work

35

A prayer can be as short or long as you want. Sometimes, it's just a thought or connection. For example, at times you may be so busy that you only have a moment to look up and say "thanks" or "help."

"One single grateful thought
toward heaven is the most
perfect prayer!"

G. E. LESSING, GERMAN CRITIC AND
DRAMATIST, 1729–1781

36

Thank God for your health just before exercising.

health

37

While shaving, ask God to make you a more loving person.

38

Do you feel like you get your sense of identity from your job, spouse, family, money, or friends? Ask God to build your sense of purpose and meaning through your relationship with Him instead.

39

Pray for a co-worker or family member while you are putting on your shoes in the morning.

others

40

As your children get on the school bus, ask God to watch over them while they are away. Pray that they will be kind to others and make wise choices.

"I remember my mother's prayers and they have always followed me. They have clung to me all my life."

ABRAHAM LINCOLN,
US PRESIDENT, 1809–1865

41

When washing your hands, ask God to make you a better spouse, parent, sibling, son, or daughter.

"I will sprinkle clean water on you, and you will be clean; I will cleanse you from all your impurities and from all your idols."

EZEKIEL 36:25

42

Sometimes life brings situations too painful to pray for in great detail. God knows what is happening—just tell Him you're hurting. Ask for His mercy.

Late nineteenth-century pastor Charles Spurgeon, author of over two hundred books, who regularly preached to over ten thousand people in London every Sunday (before microphones were invented), used prayer to cope with his frequent bouts of depression. He expressed his anguish directly to God.

43

At night while brush-
ing your teeth, thank
God for three things
that happened
during your day.

reflection

44

When you are faced with an especially big problem that completely overwhelms you, write it down on paper and visually hand it over to God. Sometimes, people will place that paper into a fire to symbolize the problem being out of their hands and into God's.

"I sit beside my lonely fire
And pray for wisdom yet:
For calmness to remember
Or courage to forget."

CHARLES HAMILTON AÏDÉ,
FRENCH-ENGLISH NOVELIST AND
MUSICIAN, 1826–1906

45

Before eating, thank God for providing the meal set before you.

provision

46

There are no coincidences in your life. Thank God for those small miracles He surprises you with each day.

"Prayer is
The world in tune,
A spirit-voice,
And vocal joys,
Whose echo is heaven's bliss."

HENRY VAUGHAN,
WELSH POET, 1621–1695

47

Just before meeting
a friend for lunch, ask
God to strengthen
your relationship with
him or her.

48

Ask God to help you be patient when you are experiencing frustration with technology and you can't figure out how to fix it.

49

Have a difficult person in your life? Whether it be a manager, co-worker, spouse, or friend, ask God to help you to see that person as He does.

"Prayer does not change God,
but changes him who prays."

ege

SØREN KIERKEGAARD,
DANISH PHILOSOPHER, 1813–1855

50

While working in your
yard, thank God for
the beautiful world
He created.

beauty

51

When looking through social media and feeling pulled to compare your life to another's, ask God to help you view yourself through His eyes.

"The LORD your God is with you,
the Mighty Warrior who saves.
He will take great delight in you;
in his love he will
no longer rebuke you,
but will rejoice over you
with singing."

ZEPHANIAH 3:17

52

When saying goodbye to your spouse or significant other, ask God to give him or her wisdom and prudence.

goodbyes

53

When in deep turmoil and despair, the psalmist poured his heart out before God (Psalm 102).

"I call on the LORD in my distress, and he answers me."

PSALM 120:1

54

Feeling uncertain? King Solomon, the wisest man who ever lived, wrote, "In all your ways submit to him, and he will make your paths straight." —Proverbs 3:6 (Note: This doesn't say "smooth," it says "straight.")

When asked if she was ever discouraged, Mother Teresa (1910–1997) answered, "I do not pray for success, I ask for faithfulness."

FROM A NEW YORK TIMES
INTERVIEW, JUNE 18, 1980

55

Take a walk outside and invite God to come with you. Speak to Him, aloud or silently, and thank Him for the beauty He has created. Calm your spirit and be open to anything He might convey to you.

engage

56

In the shower, don't just clean your outside, cleanse your soul as well. Ask God to search your heart—see if there's anything for which you need to ask His forgiveness.

57

When you are tempted to distract yourself from life's problems, instead of turning to social media or surfing the Internet, ask God to strengthen and guide you through your difficulties.

58

When hearing news about the president, prominent world leaders, or other government officials, ask God to give them wisdom, integrity, and conviction.

"Pray for the Liberty of the Conscience to revive among us."

JAMES MADISON,
US PRESIDENT, 1751–1836

"I have never been disappointed when I asked in a humble and sincere way for God's help. I pray often."

JIMMY CARTER,
US PRESIDENT, B. 1924

"I pray to God that I shall not live one hour after I have thought of using deception."

QUEEN ELIZABETH I,
ENGLISH MONARCH, 1533–1603

59

Ask God to watch over you when starting your car or stepping into a bus, train, or cab.

protection

60

Not sure what to call God? Christ always, except once just before His death, referred to God as "Father." This illustrates God's desire to have a personal, intimate relationship with us.

"Whoever in prayer can say, 'Our Father,' acknowledges and should feel the brotherhood of the whole race of mankind."

TRYON EDWARDS,
AMERICAN THEOLOGIAN, 1809–1894

61

Every time you reach for your TV remote, ask God for discernment in guarding what comes into your home.

discernment

62

When you feel lonely, thank God that He is with you. Think of three other things to thank Him for.

63

Ask for wisdom managing
your money when
reconciling your bank
account or paying your bills.

64

As you watch your child sleep, pray for him or her to develop a close and loving relationship with God.

Trust

65

When riding in an elevator, ask to be forgiven for an unkind act you did that day.

"If we confess our sins, he is faithful and just and will forgive us our sins and purify us from all unrighteousness."

1 JOHN 1:9

66

If you are in a public place but want to connect to God, hum a song of praise to Him. If you live in a big city, you can pray aloud—no one will look twice!

connection

67

Give thanks to God when your children are obedient, especially if it's an issue in which you've been working with them for a long time.

"Do not pray for gold and jade and precious things; pray that your children and grandchildren may all be good."

CHINESE PROVERB

68

As you arrive home and walk through your front door, thank God for getting you through the day.

69

Ask God to help you be a cheerful giver when receiving your paycheck or paystub.

70

If you are blessed with an active imagination and cannot pray silently without becoming distracted, write your prayers in a journal.

Dear God,
Thank you for
giving me hope

focus

71

When you feel upset by something a friend or family member posts online, ask God to help you seek truth and peace.

72

While washing your face in the morning, thank God for the talents He has given you. Ask Him to help you use these gifts to assist or uplift others.

73

After making a purchase, give thanks to God for meeting your physical needs as you put your wallet or phone away.

"And my God will meet all your needs according to the riches of his glory in Christ Jesus."

PHILIPPIANS 4:19

74

Pray for courage when you feel afraid. Request the strength to face the fear, as a step toward maturity, instead of leaving the fear unaddressed.

I lift up my eyes to the mountains—
    where does my help come from?
My help comes from the Lord,
    the Maker of heaven and earth.
He will not let your foot slip—
    he who watches over you will not
        slumber;
indeed, he who watches over Israel
    will neither slumber nor sleep.
The Lord watches over you—
    the Lord is your shade at your right
        hand;
the sun will not harm you by day,
    nor the moon by night.
The Lord will keep you from all harm—
    he will watch over your life;
the Lord will watch over your coming and
        going
    both now and forevermore.

PSALM 121

75

Pray with someone.
You can do this in
person, via video chat,
or on the phone.

community

76

While waiting in line, ask God to help you think of others as more important than yourself. Remember that people are the highest form of God's creation.

"Whoever is patient has great
understanding,
but one who is quick-tempered
displays folly."

PROVERBS 14:29

77

When you anticipate a stressful day ahead, set an alarm to go off periodically to remind you to pray.

reminders

78

Commit your day to God on your commute to work or school in the morning. Or, if you're like me and work from home, pray on your way from bed to the computer.

"For we are co-workers in God's service; you are God's field, God's building."

1 CORINTHIANS 3:9

79

Need a quiet, peaceful place to pray? Go to a nearby church, temple, or synagogue and talk to God there.

80

Not sure God hears your prayers? Ask to be humbled. This type of prayer is usually very quickly answered—for me within twenty-four hours. It's never pleasant, but in the long run I'm always a better person because of it.

81

Bow your head
before God. Imagine
approaching Him at
His heavenly throne.

worship

82

Remember, when praying, no topic is off-limits. God already knows everything happening in your heart, so you can talk to Him about anything.

"Do not be anxious about anything, but in every situation, by prayer and petition, with thanksgiving, present your requests to God."

PHILIPPIANS 4:6

83

When walking up a
flight of stairs, with
each step tell God
one thing you are
thankful for.

Thanks

84

If you are unsure what to pray for in a certain situation, requests for strength and wisdom are always good choices.

85

When experiencing
a miracle, relay your
sense of awe to
God. Tell Him how
amazing He is.

86

Thank God for the joy He brings you through special relationships.

joy

87

At the doctor's or dentist's office, pray while you sit in the waiting room.

88

Be persistent in prayer. In times of deep longing, Job of the Old Testament never stopped asking God for relief.

89

Gaze at the sky and admire God's beauty. Praise Him for His majesty.

90

When you are a passenger in a car, bus, train, or taxi, go over in your mind things you will do at your destination. Pray for God's hand over each activity.

91

When exercising, ask God to watch over you, clear your mind, and help you focus on Him.

exercise

92

While you get dressed in the morning, thank God for the body He uniquely created for you.

The Roman poet and satirist Juvenal (AD 55–127) said to pray for a sound mind in a sound body.

93

Do you know a family member or friend who is in pain? Ask that you can be a comfort to him or her.

comfort

94

On the way to meet a friend, ask God to open your heart to what He would have you learn from this person.

When you have extra time to pray for friends and family, you can pray for someone whose name begins with "A," then "B," and go through the alphabet.

95

When you are going through a challenging situation, thank God for the character He is building in your life.

"Let us not become weary in doing good, for at the proper time we will reap a harvest if we do not give up."

GALATIANS 6:9

96

Talk to God aloud
while driving in the car.
Try telling Him how
your day is going.

communication

97

When checking into a hotel, ask God to be with you, watch over you, and keep you close to Him.

"The LORD will watch over
your coming and going
both now and forevermore."

PSALM 121:8

98

If you think it may be self-centered to pray for something, do it anyway. If you are being selfish, the best way for God to let you know is through direct communication with Him. If you are praying for the wrong things, He will show you what is important to focus on. The point is—don't avoid praying!

persistence

99

When turning your car off, thank God for a safe journey.

100

Facing the most difficult task of His life, Jesus Christ prayed that the Father's will, not His, be done.

In his letter to friends in Ephesus, Paul wrote, "May you be able to feel and understand, as all God's children should, how long, how wide, how deep, and how high his love really is; and to experience this love for yourselves, though it is so great that you will never see the end of it or fully know or understand it."

EPHESIANS 3:18–19 TLB

101

Ask God to show Himself and His love to you. Over the next few days, watch for a response.

ACKNOWLEDGMENTS

Thank you, Carrie Rosema, for the beautiful photography in this book. During all those late-night pizza parties in our collegiate dorm rooms, who could have imagined we'd create a book together? And that nearly twenty years after the first edition, when we ran around New York City in the rain finding and capturing the most stunning images, we'd partner together again? I'm forever grateful to you for dedicating your time and talents to this project.

Thank you, Chriscynethia Floyd and Katara Patton for your wonderful support. And thanks to all the rest of the Our Daily Bread Publishing team, including Patti Brinks, Dawn Anderson, Sarah De Mey, and Linnae Conkel.

Thank you to my amazing friends who offered invaluable input, advice, and encouragement: Liz Balmer, Hallie Bandy, Peter Bishai, Ginny Blakely, Lora Gaston, Kevin Huggins, David Murray, Amy Newman, Kimi Price Queguiner, Jeremy Schieffelin, and Michael Shubra.

Thank you to IBM for flying me to Asia and Australia twelve times in the early 2000s—giving me time to write the majority of this book. You and our spinoff, Kyndryl, have brought me opportunities beyond my wildest imagination.

Thank you, Mom, for your suggestions and encouragement. You always make me feel as if I can succeed at anything I put my mind to.

Sally, it was Aristotle who said, "What is a friend? A single soul dwelling in two bodies." How much more of a sister. Thank you for being such a rock in my life.

My dear Lee and Adeline, you embody the most beautiful answers to my deepest prayers.

Joanne